Your Words Matter
The Power of Words

Dr. La'Chandra C. Parker

Cover design by: K&T Graphics

Edited by: Critique Editing Services

i

Dedication

Your Words Matter is dedicated to my former self and any other woman who has ever struggled with speaking truthfully through positive words. Positive words produce good fruit, negative words destroy.

Acknowledgments

I first and foremost thank GOD for without Him giving me the vision, this would not have been possible.

I thank my husband, my number one cheerleader, for pushing me and encouraging me to get this project done. He always pushes me to excel and I couldn't have gotten it done without him. He corrects me and makes me better.

I acknowledge my God-ordained friendship with my sister-friend, Ashley Thompson-Moran. In the short time we have known each other, you have blessed me with encouraging words, advice, and spoken words of life to me during the process of writing this book. You provided me an ear, gave me the word of the Lord, and helped me hold myself accountable.

Thank you.

Foreword

As women we many times are defined by other's standards. We can often forget who we are and what God's purpose is for us.

La'Chandra gives us a daily word to help us define and affirm who we are individually and collectively as women no matter where we're from and what we believe. We are made in His image and no good thing will be withheld from us.

Rev. Ashley A. Thompson-Moran

Ashley Thompson-Moran, MA, ABD

Introduction

This book was inspired by a Words Work Wonders Women's Facebook group, developed by Karen B. Moore. At the time, I was in a state of reflection and evaluation of my life and praying to God to clearly hear His voice, to truly know and understand my purpose. During this time God provided the answers I was seeking through the words He gave me daily during the 30 day Words Work Wonders Series.

I pray this book helps you to choose your words wisely, as they are so important. Put into practice speaking positive words to assist you in living a positive life, and watch your life change.

Table of Contents

Day 1
Sound

The word sound is defined in the dictionary as vibrations that travel through the air or another medium and can be heard when they reach a person's ear.

God is listening to our prayers and whatever we ask in His name He will fulfill. He comes to us in subtle, sometimes unusual ways. When He does this He is working on teaching us to be in tune to Him.

Has the sound you hear when He is speaking to you been unusual in any way? Lately for me, His sound has shown up in an unusual way, to grab my attention and to get me positioned for what He is getting ready to do for me.

I hear the sound of victory! Thank you, God for the victory.

What sound do you hear? Think on that question and begin to send up the advance praise, for victory belongs to you.

Day 2
New

The dictionary definition of the word new is not existing before; made, introduced, or discovered recently or now for the first time.

Today is a new day, never seen before. It is a day to do something you have never done, engage in something you have never engaged in, create something. Get it yet? Do something new!

Oftentimes we have ideas, dreams, etc., that we never act upon, but that is not what God intends for us. He creates all things new and that thing you have inside of you, that's right, that new thing, He is waiting for you to grab hold of it and move!

Lately I have been moving on some new things that GOD gave me to do. I am so excited about the future. I know change can be uncomfortable sometimes, but it is necessary to birth the new!

Today I encourage you to work on whatever your new thing is. Once you take the first step, God will handle the rest!

Day 3
Renew

Renew defined by Merriam-Webster means to make like new: restore to freshness, vigor, or perfection; to make new spiritually.

God has renewed my strength, faith, love, hope, peace, and joy! I am a different person, I am renewed!

My prayer is that God renews you!

Be blessed~

Day 4
Truth

The dictionary defines truth as the quality or state of being true; that which is true or in accordance with fact or reality.

Why does being truthful hurt some people? The saying "tell the truth and shame the devil," I guess goes hand in hand with describing those the truth hurts.

I have always been direct, as I do not see the need to not be truthful with people. Sometimes it has not been received well, sometimes it has been received well. You see people say they want the truth, but in actuality there are those who would rather get a false depiction of the truth.

You see God deals in truth. His word is true and will not return void. So why do so many walk around in a web of lies? I cannot and will not sacrifice myself or anyone I love by living in a web of lies. I live in truth, it's the only way to live!

If people can't be truthful with me/you, there is no need to be in communion with them. No love lost, it's just that my/your truth and their lies just won't mix.

Are you living in your truth?

Day 5
Displacement

Merriam-Webster defines the word displacement as the act or process of displacing: the state of being displaced.

In order for God to get you into the perfect place, He creates displacement. At the time the displacement happens, we may be in a state of shock, bewilderment, or surprise because we don't understand what is going on. When this happens, it is just a part of the growing process, so do not be dismayed.

I am in a state of Divine Displacement and on the other side, I will see the future God has planned for me.

Get in order to be displaced to get to the appropriate place God has for you.

Day 6
Protect

Protect as defined by the dictionary means to keep safe from harm or injury; to provide a guard or shield.

Protecting my peace is so very important to me at this point in my life. God gives me peace in the midst of the storm when the enemy tries to rear his ugly head; He will give you peace as well!

If something threatens to disturb your peace, get rid of it, don't indulge in it, move on. There are too many blessings attached to you, so don't jeopardize them by allowing things/people to disturb your peace.

Protect your peace!

Are you protecting your peace?

Day 7
Past

The dictionary defines past as time gone by; something that happened or was done in the past.

Do not look back and dwell on your past. Thank God for moving you beyond your past. It's over and can't be revisited or changed, so don't allow people to drag you back to that place.

Let the past be.

Are there some things in your past that you need to let go of or release? Write those things below and declare to God you will leave them in the pages of this book, releasing them from your thoughts.

_____

_____

_____

_____

_____

_____

Day 8
Answer

The act in reaction to (a sound, such as a phone ringing or a knock or ring on a door); say or write something to deal with or as a reaction to someone or something is the definition of the word answer according to Merriam-Webster dictionary.

Everything said/told doesn't need to be justified with an answer, especially when it is something that could possibly disrupt one's peace. There is only one who deserves an answer at all times and that is my/our God.

My answer is yes!

Day 9
Grateful

Grateful is defined in the dictionary as a feeling or showing an appreciation of kindness; thankful.

This year I am most grateful that God has continued to give me grace, mercy, and favor!

Just like the inspiring words to the song "Grateful" by Hezekiah Walker, I am grateful for everything God has done and continues to do for me. I am grateful that He continues to bless me time and time again, even when I don't deserve it.

I am so GRATEFUL!!

What are some things you are grateful for? Take a moment to create a list below:

_____

_____

_____

_____

_____

_____

Day 10
Motive

The dictionary defines motive as a reason for doing something, especially one that is hidden or not obvious.

I have experienced disappointment in those I felt would have my back in times of need. It was disappointing and hurtful to learn someone I have held down did not do the same for me. When this happens I give it to God and ask Him to create in me a clean heart and ask that He helps me to not hold onto the hurt. When someone shows me who they are, I see them.

You see my motives for doing something for someone are never to receive the glory or recognition. My motives come from a genuine place, to be a blessing to/for someone in a time of need. My prayer is for others to do the same always. Let's not get caught up. Do not have non-genuine motives in doing things for/to others.

God knows our hearts. This is a "motive" check. Are your motives pure or are they dirty?

Oh Bless His Name!

Day 11
Invest

Invest is defined by Merriam-Webster as a means to make use of for future benefits or advantages; to involve or engage, especially emotionally.

More and more I have been reflecting on the things I invest my time in. I have learned that whatever I invest my time in will grow because that is where my focus lies.

In my time with God this morning, invest was within the reading and it stood out to me. I thought about how investing time with God is necessary in order to grow spiritually, emotionally, and physically. We can attempt to do things in our own strength, but if He is not in it, it will be difficult. I reavow that I will invest my time with Him even more because He has been so good to me!

I invest pieces of myself in many different activities, but the activity most important to invest myself in is spending time with God and growing myself to be a blessing to others.

Think about how you invest your time today and remember the greatest time we can invest is our time with God.

Day 12
Give

The word give is defined in the dictionary as freely transferring the possession of (something) to (someone); hand over to.

Today I pose two simple questions: Are you a cheerful giver? In what ways do you give?

God gives to us freely and His word never returns void. I am so thankful for that very thing. He changed me and set me on the giving path. There was a time I was not a giver, but when you know better, you do better! Something to think about.

"Every man according as he purposeth in his heart, so let him give; not grudgingly, or of necessity: for God loveth a cheerful giver."

(2 Corinthians 9:7 KJV)

Be blessed~

Day 13
Grace

Simple elegance or refinement of movement; courteous goodwill defines what grace is, according to the dictionary.

As I pondered on this word today, I was reminded of several situations I had been in recently where old slew-footed Lucifer tried to show his head to get a reaction out of me, using others. When I tell you I handled those situations with the grace God gave me without flinching, they didn't even know how to react.

You see people will try so hard to bring you out of your character, but my God won't allow you to, even when you want to, when you are sincerely trying to live right and do God's will.

He tells us His grace is sufficient and it most certainly is. There was a time I didn't know how to utilize the grace He bestowed upon me; those times are long gone, oh bless His name. Anything coming to disturb my peace must make a u-turn! With the strength of God, I am not entertaining it.

Oh happy day to be able to move gracefully!

Day 14
Hear

I define the word hear as giving one's attention to a sound; an act of listening to something.

I listen intently to hear what God is saying to me. Sometimes my hearing is blocked by extraneous noise. Why, I am not quite sure, but when I get still and focus, I hear clearly the message my God is sending to me. I continuously pray for Him to speak to me and allow me to know without a doubt it's His voice. I only want to hear His voice, for I know He will not lead me astray.

This scripture gives me comfort, for it is forever true.

"So then faith cometh by hearing, and hearing by the word of God."

(Romans 10:17 KJV)

What you put into your hearing will nourish you or stunt you. I choose nourishment.

Be blessed~

Day 15
Faith

Faith means you have complete trust or confidence in someone or something; strong belief in God or in the doctrines of a religion, based on spiritual apprehension rather than proof, as defined by Merriam-Webster.

If 2020 has taught me nothing else, it has taught me that we must keep the FAITH. We must keep the FAITH when things seem impossible. God has proven Himself to me and my family through this pandemic. We have been blessed above and beyond, and it is because we have kept the FAITH!

It has not been easy, but we have done it! He has been so faithful, and I am grateful. God will keep His promises. Activate your faith if you are wavering, you will not be disappointed!

"And whatever you ask in prayer, you will receive, if you have faith."

(Matthew 21:22)

I am a witness, it is so!

Day 16
Bond

One definition of bond in the dictionary is a relationship between people or groups based on shared feelings, interests, or experiences; a connection between two surfaces or objects that have been joined together, especially by means of an adhesive substance, heat, or pressure.

There are times in our lives when we are bonded to people, places, and things that are not good for us. Although we know it, we continue trying to cultivate that bond, only to in the end have to break it. Most times when that bond is broken, it brings pain, discomfort, and/or sadness.

I am here today to tell you of a bond that is not easily broken and that is the one you share with your heavenly Father. He will loose shackles and set you free, and I am so glad about that! I am bonded with my GOD who loves me unconditionally, and He gave me the strength and authority to loose those bonds that mean me no good.

Day 17
Clean

Clean is defined in the dictionary as something being free from dirt, marks, or stains.

Daily I pray and ask God to create in me a clean heart and renew a right spirit within me. If we take in all of the trash that we encounter on a daily basis, our hearts can become stained/dirty. God did not create us to walk around with stained/dirty hearts.

How many of us can say that we have been guilty of allowing people, situations, and circumstances to dirty up our hearts? I have been guilty. The older I get, the wiser I become and if something disrupts my peace, I walk away from it.

I challenge you all to take a self-evaluation to see if there are some people, things, situations, and/or circumstances that you are a part of that could create in you a dirty, marked, or stained heart. If there are, let them go quickly, and cry out to God to clean your heart.

The heart is made of love and anything dealing with love; I just believe it is meant to be clean, what about you?

Is your heart clean?

Day 18
Judgment

Judgment defined by Merriam-Webster is the process of forming an opinion or evaluation by discerning and comparing.

How many of us have passed judgment on someone, something, etc? I will be the first to say I am guilty. I am not proud to say that I have judged others on so many occasions. I ask God for forgiveness and pray He will take away the urge to judge. Take it away, God!

"For we must all appear before the judgment seat of Christ, so that each one may receive what is due for what he has done in the body, whether good or evil."

(2 Corinthians 5:10)

I will do good, not evil!

Day 19
Love

The dictionary defines love as an intense feeling of deep affection; a great interest and pleasure in something.

One of my pastor's sermon topics was "Give the Gift of Love." So many people use the word love so loosely. I often see posts on social media where someone professes to love another's life, or love another so big, etc., and I often sit back and ponder, do they really mean what they say or is it just the "it" thing to do for the moment?

I did not grow up hearing the word love a lot, although I knew I was loved because I was cared for, my needs were met, and I did not go lacking. As I became an adult I realized the way I had been raised to be strong and not really show love, posed an issue for me to effectively show my love for others. I thought I knew how to love, but I had so much to learn about the four-letter word.

In due time I began to understand what love was and how I could show love, just as God shows us love. I do not use that word loosely, but I strive daily to love people with the love of God even when I feel they don't deserve it. What if God didn't love us? I can't imagine how my life would be if He didn't love me.

You see our flesh will tell us to dislike people when they have wronged us, been unkind to us, lied on us, whatever the issue, but I serve a God who says to LOVE them in spite of it all. Love is patient and kind and I will be the first to admit, I didn't always love the way God tells us to. I am still a work in progress, but I am better today than I was on yesterday. Give the Gift of LOVE and be blessed because of it. LOVE is the best gift anyone can receive.

"Above all, keep loving one another earnestly, since love covers a multitude of sins."

(1 Peter 4:8)

Love More~

Day 20
Clarity

The dictionary defines clarity as the quality of being coherent and intelligible. The quality of transparency or purity.

My desire is to have 100% clarity to complete the work that God has for me to do. I want to have that same clarity in listening to hear His voice. Sometimes I know that I have too much noise around me to be able to hear from Him. I have been praying to be clear on this very thing. I want to be used by Him to be a blessing to so many.

I have always been a transparent person; what you see is what you get. At times it has not been received in the appropriate manner, however, I have grown into a different space to utilize my transparency in a more appropriate manner for those I encounter. You see my desire is to please God and I couldn't do that properly in the "old space" I occupied.

I continue to be a work in progress, but I thank God for working within me to be coherent in the process of becoming who He intends for me to be.

Day 21
Possible

Possible is defined in the dictionary as being able to be done; within the power or capacity of someone or something.

With God ALL things are possible, so why don't we walk in that very thing 100% of the time? I have been guilty of allowing doubt to creep into situations at times, but that is not what God wants for us.

"But Jesus beheld them, and said unto them, 'With men this is impossible; but with God all things are possible.'"

(Matthew 19:26 King James Version)

My sisters, today as you go about your business be reminded that with God ALL things are possible, even when it seems impossible. That thing you've been holding within, is possible. My God, I am speaking to myself...let God show you the unlimited possibilities.

Be blessed~

Day 22
Manipulate

The word manipulate meaning from the dictionary is to handle or control (a tool, mechanism, etc.), typically in a skillful manner; control or influence (a person or situation) (cleverly, unfairly, or unscrupulously).

If you have ever had an opportunity to be involved with a manipulative person, you recognize that he/she might twist what you say and make it about them, hijack the conversation or make you feel like you've done something wrong when you're not quite sure you have. He/she can be so cunning and convincing until you begin to doubt yourself, beat yourself up, and/or have a pity party; the list could go on and on.

When you stop and think about such actions, you can clearly see that a manipulative person is just like the devil. He is manipulative and will have you all jacked up if you allow it. You know the devil doesn't have any new tricks, he just uses a different person, tool, tactic, etc.

Do not allow anyone to manipulate you, your thoughts, your words, your actions! This one is personal, sisters. I pray that the spirit of manipulation will bypass you/me. I pray for those who allow the devil to use them as the "manipulator" and that they will see the error of their ways and repent.

Do not be a manipulator or allow yourself to be manipulated.

Day 23
Reflect

The dictionary defines the word reflect as to think deeply or carefully about.

Reflecting is so important in order for us to make necessary adjustments in life. If we don't reflect on ourselves, it is difficult for us to become better individuals.

In my meditation time today, I began to ponder about how I reflect upon different things, situations, etc. I began to think about the Michael Jackson song, Man in the Mirror. It immediately reminded me that each day God gives me is another day to take a look at the face in the mirror and make a conscious effort to do something good and/or be better than I was the day before.

Sometimes we don't like what we see in the mirror or what reflecting upon ourselves reveals, however, it is important to be clear in what we discover, so we are clear in our daily interactions.

"As in water face reflects face, so the heart of man reflects the man."

(Proverbs 27:19)

I leave you with this question today: What does your heart reflect?

My prayer is that God creates in us a clean heart and renews a right spirit within us, so that we reflect His everlasting love to one another!

Day 24
Trust

Trust is defined in the dictionary as a firm belief in the reliability, truth, ability, or strength of someone or something.

Anytime we are faced with trials we have the ability to choose how we will react/respond. Are we going to trust that God is working things out for our good, or are we going to try to fix it in our own strength? I choose to trust God, knowing that He has already fought and won the victory/battle just for me. There is no need to doubt His word because He will do just what He said over and over and over again.

(Proverbs 3:5-6 New International Version) says, "Trust in the Lord with all your heart and lean not to your own understanding; in all your ways submit to him, and he will make your paths straight."

Trusting in you, Lord, always!

Day 25
Joy

Joy is a feeling, expressing, or causing great pleasure and happiness, as defined in the dictionary.

Oftentimes in life many things can change your perception and/or outlook on situations that you find yourself in. How do you handle adversity when it comes? For me, going through it without getting worked up has proven to be beneficial. You see I could be stressed, but what will that do for me? Absolutely nothing. I choose joy!

"Count it all joy, my brothers, when you meet trials of various kinds, for you know that the testing of your faith produces steadfastness."

(James 1:2)

The good news is we can rejoice even in tough times, secure in our faith and in God's unconditional love.

Day 26
Surrender

Merriam-Webster's definition of surrender is yield to the power, control, or possession of another upon compulsion or demand; to give up completely or agree to forgo, especially in favor of another.

Today I simply say, I surrender all to you, God! It feels great to be able to do so! I cannot keep meddling in things I need to take my hands off of because you have it all worked out in your timing.

Is there anything you need to surrender today? If so, do it now!

List the things you will surrender today below

_____

_____

_____

_____

_____

Day 27
Disappointment

The dictionary defines the word disappointment as sadness or displeasure caused by the nonfulfillment of one's hopes or expectations.

How many times have we experienced disappointment? For me, there have been numerous times I have been disappointed by the actions of others. I have also disappointed myself by engaging in things that I had no business engaging in. When I did that I disappointed God, however, I find joy in knowing that He did not hold that against me. He granted me another opportunity/chance to get it right. So why don't we allow those people/things that disappoint us the same opportunity? Sometimes we do, sometimes we don't.

God's plan is for us to release our cares upon Him. Those disappointments are a part of those cares. You see we will have those disappointing experiences, but how we handle them will reveal who we truly are. Be a person of love despite the disappointments. I know it's easier said than done, but it has to be done.

Go through the disappointment to get to the appointment God has for you!

Be blessed~

Day 28
Release

The act of setting free or letting go is the meaning of release.

I used to be extremely selfish, believe it or not. I wanted things my way and my way only. As I've gotten older I have learned to compromise. I had to release that spirit of selfishness in order to grow into selflessness. While I continue to be a work in progress, I am a long way from where I used to be. Releasing things to God and understanding that I can't be in control of everything nor can I be selfish in dealing with things, people, etc., allows me to focus on my actions, thoughts, and intentions. I have learned to release it all to Him and He will work it out.

What things do you need to release to Him?

Day 29
Seek

To seek means to attempt to find (something), search for, defined by the dictionary.

During the COVID-19 pandemic I have been seeking God more. Oftentimes, I have attempted to do many things in my own strength. As I have grown in the word and in my walk, I totally pray and speak God's will over my life. I can do nothing without Him. I am seeking to achieve everything He has for me!

I am so excited about this journey, seeking Him more!

Day 30
Distraction

The dictionary defines the word distraction as a thing that prevents someone from giving full attention to something else; extreme agitation of the mind or emotions is the meaning of distraction.

I will not allow distractions to deter me from the things God has in store for me. The distraction is the enemy trying to keep me off focus, but it will never work. I am minimizing distractions daily.

Stay focused, my sisters, do not allow distractions to prevent you from the things God has for you!

What distractions can you identify immediately that threaten your growth in God?

Day 31
Calm

The dictionary defines the word calm as an adjective as not showing or feeling nervousness, anger, or other strong emotions.

The dictionary defines the word calm as a noun as the absence of violent or confrontational activity within a place or group.

The dictionary defines the word calm as a verb as to make (someone) tranquil and quiet; soothe.

When faced with adversity it is important to remain CALM.

When you feel like there is trouble on every side, remain CALM.

Whenever people attempt to bring you out of your character remain CALM.

You see there was a time in my life when I would cut someone down quicker than they could blink because I felt they deserved it. Back then, I didn't care whether they liked it or not, if they crossed me, it did not end well. I would go off in a second, not a care in the world. I know it was not pleasing to God, but I just couldn't let it go.

Fast forward to now, I bask in opportunities to turn the other cheek. If I see that someone or something is trying to disrupt my peace and bring me out of my CALM state, I let it go. You see I don't have time for people, places, or things that deter me from being in my CALM state. I pray fervently for God to keep me, so that I don't come out of character on so many occasions.

I do fall short daily, but it is my desire to not fall into the trap of disturbing my CALM.

God wants us to remain CALM in the midst of it all because in the end, we will reap a reward.

Are you allowing people, places, or things to disrupt your place of CALM? Don't do it, it's not worth the sacrifice.

Stay CALM and watch GOD move!

****

Our words have the power to bring life or death to situations. Choose to use words to uplift, inspire, motivate, and encourage others. What is the purpose of using words to cause harm? There is none. If we want God to bless up, we must bless others. This is why *Your Words Matter!*

I hope this book sparked something within you to get to know God better. If you do not know Him, I invite you to get to know Him. He's a life changer, a problem-solver, a mind-regulator. You will not be disappointed. So if you would like to know Him in the pardon of your sins, read the scripture below. It's just that simple.

"That if thou shalt confess with thy mouth the Lord Jesus, and shalt believe in thine heart that God hath raised from the dead, thou shalt be saved."

(Romans 10:9 KJV)

About the Author

Dr. La'Chandra C. Parker is a wife, bonus mom, educator and servant leader who believes in the word of God. She is a native of Clinton, North Carolina and resides in Newton Grove, North Carolina with her loving and devoted husband Tyrone and their yorkie Bentley and pit bull Terra. In 2020 she heard the voice of God tell her to develop this book to assist women in tailoring their words of positivity to empower, motivate, and uplift, not only for themselves but for others. In strengthening her own walk with God, she has transformed her daily words and aspirations to develop the life God intends for her to have.

Her hobbies are singing, reading, spending time with family, and watching TV. She loves God and hopes this book helps others to use their words cautiously and intentionally to grow themselves. She seeks to develop more self-help books to assist others in growing into the person God has called them to be.

www.ingramcontent.com/pod-product-compliance
Lightning Source LLC
Chambersburg PA
CBHW072024060426
42449CB00034B/2129